Cataraqui United Church Cemetery 1

The Grave Whisperer

Angeline Gallant

Published by Angeline Gallant, 2022.

CATARAQUI UNITED CHURCH CEMETERY 1

First edition. September 23, 2022.

ISBN: 979-8215698310

Written by Angeline Gallant.

Also by Angeline Gallant

Calling Her Heart

Whisper of the Heart

No Turning Back

Forsake Me Not

Hear My Cry

Keeper Of Secrets

A Lady's Secret

Midnight's Awakening

Heart of the Storm

Walking Through The Storm

Secrets of the Underworld

Deklan's Dragons

Tell My Story Collcction

Tell My Story: England 1852

The Grave Whisperer

Wedding Bells in Kingston, Ontario, Canada 1923

St. Paul's Anglican Churchyard Kingston, Ontario, Canada A-B

St. Paul's Anglican Churchyard, Kingston, Ontario, Canada C - D

St. Paul's Anglican Churchyard, Kingston, Ontario, Canada G - H

St. Paul's Anglican Churchyard, Kingston, Ontario, Canada J - N

St. Paul's Anglican Churchyard, Kingston, Ontario, Canada O - R

St. Paul's Anglican Churchyard, Kingston, Ontario, Canada S - T

St. Paul's Anglican Churchyard, Kingston, Ontario T - Z

Small Graveyards & Burial Grounds: Kingston, Ontario, Canada

Cataraqui United Church Cemetery 1

The Wolf Whisperer Series

The Cry of the Wolf

Journey of the Heart

Wolf Whisperer volumes 1 & 2

Standalone

Winds of Change vol 1-3

Watch for more at https://www.goodreads.com/author/show/19703964.Angeline_Gallant.

Table of Contents

ESTHER MABLE (SAUNDERS) APPLETON[1]

Esther was born on September 4, 1874 in Kingston, Ontario.

She was 24 years old when she married Thomas Henry Appleton on December 21, 1898 in Kingston.

Esther was 33 years old when her mother passed away in 1907.

She was 55 years old when her sister, Caroline Louise, passed away in 1930.

Esther was 70 years old when she passed away on June 15, 1945.

JOHN ALBERT APPLETON[2]

John was born in Kingston, Frontenac, Canada West, British Colonial America in 1864.

He was three years old when Ontario was founded on July 1, 1867.

John was seven years old when British Columbia joined the confederation in 1871.

He was 17 years old in 1881 and working as a clerk in Kingston.

John was 18 years old and working as a confectioner when he passed away on February 2, 1882.

JOHN CHARLES APPLETON[3]

John was christened on March 11, 1832 in Hevingham, Norfolk, England.

He was a year old when the Factory Act was passed in 1833.

John was two years old when his infant sister, Mary Ann, passed away in 1834.

He was five years old when his brother, James, passed away in 1837.

John was 11 years old when "A Christmas Carol" was first published in 1843.

He was 29 years old when he married Sarah Ann Claxton on October 3, 1861 in Kingston.

John was 35 years old when Ontario was founded on July 1, 1867.

He was Anglican and worked as a blacksmith in Kingston.

John was 50 years old when his son, John Albert, passed away in 1882.

He was 51 years old when the mining boom in Northern Ontario began in 1883.

John was 52 years old when his father passed away on August 14, 1884. His daughter, Martha Phoebe, passed away a few days later on August 27th. Three months later, John's daughter, Sarah Ann, passed away on November 10, 1884, followed by his daughter, Lillie, the following day on November 11th.

He was 54 years old when his mother passed away in 1886.

John was 60 years old when his sister, Isabella, passed away in 1892.

He was 74 years old when his sister, Maria, passed away in 1906.

John was 79 years old when his wife passed away in 1911.

He was 82 years old when WWI began in 1914.
John was 83 years old when he passed away on February 1, 1915.

LILLIE APPLETON[4]

Lillie was born in 1866.

She was a year old when Ontario was founded on July 1, 1867.

Lillie was five years old when British Columbia joined the confederation in 1871.

She was 16 years old when her brother, John Albert, passed away in 1882.

Lillie was 17 years old when the mining boom in northern Ontario began in 1883.

She was Anglican and a music teacher.

Lillie was 18 years old when her sister, Martha, Phoebe, passed away on August 27, 1884. Three months later, her sister, Sarah Ann, passed away on November 10th. Lillie passed away from Typhoid Fever the following day.

MARTHA PHOEBE APPLETON[5]

Martha was born in 1867.

She was three years old when British Columbia joined the confederation in 1871.

Martha was 14 years old when her brother, John Albert, passed away in 1882.

She was 15 years old when the mining boom in northern Ontario began in 1883.

Martha was 16 years old and working as a store clerk when she passed away from Typhoid Fever on August 27, 1884. She was Anglican.

SARAH ANN APPLETON[6]

Sarah was born on September 29, 1869 in Frontenac, Ontario.

She was a year old when British Columbia joined the confederation in 1871.

Sarah was 12 years old when her brother, John Albert, passed away in 1882.

She was 13 years old when the mining boom in northern Ontario in 1883.

Sarah was 15 years old when her sister, Martha Phoebe, passed away on August 27, 1884. She passed away three months later from Typhoid Fever on November 10, 1884, a day before her sister Lillie's death.

SARAH ANN (CLAXTON) APPLETON[7]

Sarah was born in England in 1843, the same year that "A Christmas Carol" was first published.

She was 18 years old when she married John Charles Appleton on October 3, 1861 in Frontenac, Ontario.

Sarah was 24 years old when Ontario was founded on July 1, 1867.

She was 28 years old when British Columbia joined the confederation in 1871.

Sarah was 37 years old when school attendance became mandatory for children on August 2, 1880.

She was 39 years old when her son, John Albert, passed away on February 2, 1882. Her brother, Robert, passed away two months later on April 2nd.

Sarah was 40 years old when the mining boom in northern Ontario began in 1883.

She was 41 years old when her daughter, Martha Phoebe, passed away on August 27, 1884. Her daughter, Sarah Ann, passed away on November 10th, followed by her daughter, Lillie, the following day on November 11th. All three children died from Typhoid Fever.

Sarah was 58 years old when her sister, Mary Ann, passed away in 1901.

She was 60 years old when her father passed away in 1903.

Sarah was 63 years old when she passed away on November 2, 1911.

THOMAS HERBERT "LEFTY" APPLETON[8]

Thomas was born in 1873.

He was nine years old when his brother, John Albert, passed away in 1882.

Thomas was 10 years old when the mining boom in northern Ontario began in 1883.

He was 11 years old when his sisters, Martha Phoebe, Sarah Ann, and Lillie passed away from Typhoid Fever in 1884.

Thomas was 25 years old when he married Esther Mabel Saunders on December 21, 1898.

He was 37 years old when The Mann Act was passed in 1910,

Thomas was 38 years old when his mother passed away in 1911.

He was 42 years old when his father passed away in 1915.

Thomas was 61 years old when the Dionne Quintuplets were born in 1934.

He was 64 years old when his brother, Samuel, passed away in 1937.

Thomas was 70 years old when his brother, Norman, passed away in 1943.

He was 72 years old when his wife passed away in 1945.

Thomas was 76 years old when his brother, George Tenor, passed away in 1949.

He was 77 years old when he passed away in 1950.

UNKNOWN ARSENETH[9]

The gravestone is very worn making it difficult to read the information, therefore it is unknown when they were born or died. More research is needed if you'd like to help.

DUNHAM ASH[10]

Dunham was born in the USA in 1811.

He was a year old when the War of 1812 took place.

Dunham was 52 years old when British Columbia joined the confederation in 1871.

He was 68 years old when he passed away on January 24, 1879. Dunham was German and Evangelical Methodist.

MARGARET (BREDEN) ASH[11]

Margaret was born in Ireland in 1811.

She was 39 years old when the Irish Potato Famine took place in 1845.

Margaret was 57 years old when the Battle of Gettysburg took place in 1863.

She was 73 years old when her husband passed away in 1879.

Margaret was 84 years old when the Women's Suffrage began in 1890.

She was 88 years old when she passed away on December 24, 1893.

ALICE JANE (ASHLEY) CHADWICK[12]

Alice was born in 1849.

She was 18 years old when Ontario was founded on July 1, 1867.

Alice was 22 years old when British Columbia joined the confederation in 1871.

She was 30 years old when she married William Miles Chadwick on December 3, 1879 in Kingston.

Alice was 34 years old when the mining boom in northern Ontario began in 1883.

She was 38 years old when her mother passed away in 1887.

Alice was 47 years old when her husband passed away in 1896.

She was 57 years old when Ontario Hydro was established in 1906.

Alice was 73 years old when she passed away on December 19, 1921.

ELIZA (ASHLEY) CHADWICK[13]

Eliza was born in 1859.

She was eight years old when Ontario was founded on July 1, 1867.

Eliza was 12 years old when British Columbia joined the confederation.

She was 64 years old when she passed away in 1923.

ELIZABETH (BURNETT) ASHLEY[14]

Elizabeth was born in 1802.

She was 18 years old when she married John William Ashley on February 17, 1820 in Kingston, Ontario.

Elizabeth was 35 years old when she passed away on June 13, 1837.

JOHN ASHLEY[15]

John passed away on January 12, 1802.

JOHN WILLIAM ASHLEY ESQ.[16]

Based on the inscription on his gravestone, John would have been born in 1799.

He was nine years old when the Atlantic slave trade was abolished in 1808.

John was 21 years old when he married Elizabeth Burnett on February 17, 1820 in Kingston, Ontario.

He was 36 years old when his brother James passed away in 1835. His father passed away on March 22nd. His brother, Frederick Henry, passed away four months later on July 30th.

John was 38 years old when his wife passed away on June 13, 1837.

He was 41 years old when he married Margaret Chrysier in 1840. His mother passed away that same year.

John was 48 years old when his brothers, George William and Adam, passed away in 1847.

He was 56 years old when his sister, Mary Ann, passed away in 1855.

John was 59 years old when he passed away on September 27, 1858.

NORA (ASHLEY) HOGAN[17]

Nora was born in 1848.

She was 19 years old when Ontario was founded on July 1, 1867.

Nora was 23 years old when British Columbia joined the confederation in 1871.

She was 80 years old when she passed away in 1928.

CLARE BERTRAM ASSELSTINE[18]

Clare was born on February 4, 1914 in Portsmouth, Frontenac, Ontario.

He was 12 years old when he accidentally drowned in the Cataraqui River in Kingston, Ontario on August 29, 1926.

HARRIET JANE (FLEMING) ASSELSTINE[19]

Harriet was born on Amherst Island, Ontario on August 27, 1871.

She was eight years old when her brother, William James, passed away in 1880.

Harriet was 11 years old when the mining boom in Northern Ontario began in 1883.

She was 18 years old when her sister, Elizabeth, passed away in 1891.

Harriet was 24 years old when she married Arthur James Asselstine on November 6, 1895 on Amherst Island.

She was 25 years old when her mother passed away in 1897.

Harriet was 27 years old when her father passed away in 1898.

She was 34 years old when Ontario Hydro was established in 1906.

Harriet was 41 years old when her brother, George Briden, passed away in 1912.

She was 46 years old when her sister, Georgia Emma Amelia, passed away in 1917. Eight months later, her son, Lawrence Wilfred, passed away on June 27, 1918.

Harriet was 52 years old when her daughter, Evelyn Mae, passed away in 1924.

She was 55 years old when her sister, Agnes, passed away in 1926.

Harriet was 57 years old when her sister, Deborah Caroline, passed away in 1928.

She was 62 years old when the Dionne Quintuplets were born in 1934.

Harriet was 80 years old when her husband passed away in 1952.

She was 88 years old when her sister, Margaret Fleming, passed away in 1960.

Harriet was 100 years old when she passed away in 1972. She was Irish and Methodist.

MARGARET LOUISA (JACKSON) ASSELSTINE[20]

Margaret was born in Ontario in 1880. She was German.

She was 10 years old when the Women's Suffrage movement began in 1890.

Margaret was 11 years old when her father passed away in 1891.

She was 19 years old when her mother passed away in 1899.

Margaret was 26 years old when she married Percy Gordon Asselstine on November 20, 1906 in Kingston, Ontario.

She was 34 years old when her sister, Lydia Helen, passed away in 1914.

Margaret was 46 years old when her son, Clare Betram, drowned on August 28, 1926.

She was 51 years old when her brother, Alfred Russell, passed away in 1951.

Margaret was 74 years old when her sister, Florella, passed away in 1954.

She was 80 years old when her husband passed away in 1960.

Margaret was 85 years old when her sister, Susan, passed away in 1965.

She was 94 years old when she passed away in 1974. Margaret was Primitive Methodist, then later, Free Methodist.

PERCY GORDON ASSELSTINE[21]

Percy was born in Napanee, Ontario on June 12, 1884.

He was 22 years old when he married Margaret Louisa Jackson on November 20, 1906 in Kingston, Ontario.

Percy was 23 years old when the Bureau of Investigation was formed in 1908.

He was 42 years old when his son, Clare Bertram, drowned on August 28, 1926.

Percy was 46 years old when both of his parents passed away in 1931.

He was 70 years old when the General Motors Auto Workers Strike took place in 1955.

Percy was 75 years old when he passed away in 1960. He was Methodist and a baker.

FRANCES ATKINS[22]

Frances passed away on January 4, 1833.

ANN ATKINSON[23]

Ann was 18 years old when she passed away on July 16, 1816.

ALEY ETTA (SILVER) AYLESWORTH[24]

Aley was born on April 16, 1868 in Ernestown, Ontario. She was Dutch.

She was two years old when British Columbia joined the confederation in 1871.

Aley was 10 years old when her brother, John, passed away in 1879.

She was 14 years old when the mining boom in northern Ontario began in 1883.

Aley was 15 years old when her father passed away in 1884.

She was 19 years old when she married John Ayelsworth on December 24, 1887.

Aley was 33 years old when her brother, William, passed away in 1901.

She was 37 years old when Ontario Hydro was established in 1906.

Aley was 39 years old when her mother passed away in 1908.

She was 40 years old when her husband passed away in 1909.

Aley was 42 years old when her sister, Louisa, passed away in 1911.

She was 51 years old when her son, Norval Clarence, passed away in 1920.

Aley was 59 years old when her brother, James Edward, passed away in 1927.

She was 74 years old when the Conservative Party won the Ontario election in 1943.

Aley was 77 years old when she passed away on April 28, 1945. She was Methodist.

JOHN ALBERT ALYESWORTH[25]

John was born on March 15, 1869 in Odessa, Ontario.

He was 13 years old when the mining boom in northern Ontario began in 1883.

John was 18 years old when he married Aley Etta Silver who was a year older than him on December 24, 1887.

He was 20 years old when the Women's Suffrage Movement began in 1890.

John was 36 years old when Ontario Hydro was established in 1906.

He was 39 years old when the NAACP was formed in 1909.

John was 40 years old when he passed away on March 13, 1909. He was Dutch and Methodist.

JOHN ALBERT AYLESWORTH II[26]

John was born in Ontario in 1918.

He was 16 years old when the Dionne Quintuplets were born in 1934.

John was 54 years old when his mother passed away in 1972.

He was 55 years old when his father passed away in 1973.

John was 64 years old when the Canada Act was passed in 1982.

He was 83 years old when he passed away on June 16, 2001.

LESTER FLOYD AYLESWORTH[27]

Lester was born on February 21, 1928.

He was a month old when he passed away on March 27, 1928.

MARY ROSETTA (ZURBRIGG) AYLESWORTH[28]

Mary was born in South Grimsby, Ontario, on March 10, 1892.

In 1901 she was nine years old and living in Wentworth, Ontario.

Mary was 13 years old when Ontario Hydro was established in 1906.

She was 17 years old when the Mann Act was passed in 1911.

Mary was 19 years old when the Girl Scouts were founded in 1912.

She was 21 years old when her mother passed away in 1913.

Mary was 22 years old when she married Wilbert Ross Aylesworth on March 10, 1914 in Kingston, Ontario.

She was 39 years old when her sister, Anna Barbara, passed away in 1931.

Mary was 54 years old when her sister, Levina, passed away in 1947.

She was 71 years old when her sister, Mary Ida, passed away in 1963.

Mary was 79 years old when she passed away in 1972. She was German and Methodist.

NANCY MERCER (DAVID) AYLESWORTH[29]

Nancy was born in Kingston, Ontario on February 15, 1853.

She was 13 years old when Ontario was founded on July 1, 1867.

Nancy was 29 years old when the mining boom in northern Ontario began in 1883.

She was 32 years old when her sister, Matilda, passed away in 1886.

Nancy was 46 years old when her father passed away in 1899.

She was 47 years old when her sister, Charlotte Mary, passed away in 1900.

Nancy was 50 years old when her mother passed away in 1903.

She was 52 years old when Ontario Hydro was established in 1906.

Nancy was 59 years old when her brother, William, passed away in 1912.

She was 76 years old when her sister, Emily, passed away in 1929.

Nancy was 82 years old when she passed away in 1936.

NORVAL CLARENCE AYLESWORTH[30]

Norval was born in Ontario in 1896.

He was 10 years old when Ontario Hydro was established in 1906.

Norval was 13 years old when his father passed away in 1909.

He was 19 years old when he married Margaret Matilda David on April 3, 1915 in Kingston, Ontario.

He was 24 years old when he passed away on February 17, 1920 in Kaladar, Ontario. He is buried with his parents in Kingston.

RANDALL ROSS AYLESWORTH[31]

Randall was born in 1954 and passed away in 1955.

WILBERT ROSS "W. R." AYLESWORTH[32]

Wilbert was born on July 14, 1892 in Kingston, Ontario. He was Dutch.

He was 13 years old when Ontario Hydro was founded in 1906. Wilbert was Methodist at the time.

Wilbert was 16 years old when his father passed away in 1909.

He was 21 years old when he married Margaret Rosetta Zurbrigg on March 10, 1914 in Kingston, Ontario.

Wilbert was 27 years old when his brother, Norval Clarence, passed away in 1920.

He served as a member of the Conservative Party for a number of years.[33]

Wilbert was 41 years old when the Dionne Quintuplets were born in 1934.

He was 47 years old when he immigrated to New York in 1940.

Wilbert was 52 years old when his mother passed away in 1945.

He was 55 years old when his brother, Rupert, passed away in 1947.

Wilbert was 69 years old when his brother, Floyd John, passed away in 1962.

He was 79 years old when his wife passed away in 1972.

Wilbert was 80 years old when he passed away in 1973.

ARTHUR FREDERICKSON BABCOCK[34]

Arthur was born on August 14, 1914 in Frontenac, Ontario.

He was 11 years old when his father passed away in 1925.

Arthur was 19 years old when the Dionne Quintuplets were born in 1934.

He was 28 years old when the Conservative Party won the Ontario elections in 1943.

Arthur was 37 years old when his mother passed away in 1952.

He was 52 years old when he passed away in 1967.

MARY EVELYN (DAY) BABCOCK[35]

Mary was born on October 13, 1907 in Kingston.

She was less than a year old when her infant sister, Bay, passed away in 1908.

Mary was 5 years old when her sister, Phyllis Irene, passed away in 1913.

She was 26 years old when the Dionne Quintuplets were born in 1934.

Mary was 44 years old when her mother passed away in 1952.

She was 59 years old when her husband, Arthur Frederickson Babcock, passed away in 1967.

Mary was 64 years old when her father passed away in 1972.

She was 74 years old when the Canada Act was passed in 1982.

Mary was 95 years old when she passed away in 2003.

ALFRED BAKER[36]

Alfred was born in England in 1882.

He was 19 years old in 1901 and working as an agricultural laborer. Alfred was living in Creacombe, Devon, England.

Alfred was 24 years old when Ontario Hydro was established in 1906.

He was 28 years old when he married Emily Maud Cairns in 1910 in Winona, Wentworth, Ontario.

Alfred was 86 years old when his wife passed away in 1968.

He was 93 years old when he passed away in 1975.

EMILY MAUD (CAIRNS) BAKER[37]

Emily was born on July 14, 1887 in Penarth, Wales.

She was five years old when her brother, Walter Frank, passed away in 1893.

Emily was 13 years old when her brother, Francis Ivor Howard, passed away in 1900.

She was 19 years old when she immigrated to Canada in 1907.

Emily was 23 years old when she married Alfred Baker on December 5, 1910 in Winona, Ontario.

She was 30 years old when her brother, Charles Ridley, passed away in 1917 in Vimy, France.

Emily was 31 years old when her brother, William John, passed away in Vimy, France in 1918.

She was 35 years old when her brother, Albert Reginald Sidney, passed away in 1923.

Emily was 38 years old when her father passed away in 1925. Her sister, Beatrice Kathleen, passed away four months later in February 1926.

She was 43 years old when her mother passed away in 1931.

Emily was 46 years old when the Dionne Quintuplets were born in 1934.

She was 63 years old when her sister, Mary, passed away in 1950.

Emily was 80 years old when she passed away on February 1, 1968. She was Anglican.

PHILLIP HENRY BAKER[38]

Phillip was born on September 8, 1882.

The mining boom in northern Ontario in 1883 before Phillip was a year old.

He was 22 years old when he married Florence Evelyn Pipe on June 7, 1905 in Kingston.

Phillip was 23 years old when Ontario Hydro was established in 1906.

He was 51 years old when the Dionne Quintuplets were born in 1934.

Philip was 57 years old when his father passed away in 1940.

He was 64 years old when his mother passed away in 1947.

Phillip was 67 years old when his brother, Eckhard Heffner, passed away in 1950.

He was 77 years old when his brother, Francis Allen, passed away in 1959. Phillip passed away four months later on April 4, 1960.

WILLIAM HARRY "HARRY" BAKER[39]

Harry was born in 1904.

He was two years old when Ontario Hydro was established in 1906. His sister, Ethel Eliza, also passed away that year.

Harry was 30 years old when the Dionne Quintuplets were born in 1934.

He was 36 years old when he married Catherine Ina Calverly in Kingston in 1956.

Harry was 72 years old when his brother, John Alfred, passed away in 1976.

He was 78 years old when he passed away on January 10, 1982.

MABEL LOUISA (DAVID) BAUDER[40]

Mabel was born on September 23, 1887 in Kingston, Ontario.

She was 15 years old when her brother, Stanley David, passed away in 1903.

Mabel was 18 years old when Ontario Hydro was established in 1906.

She was 31 years old when her mother passed away in 1919.

Mabel was 32 years old when she married Ira Nelson Bauder on August 10, 1920 in Verona, Ontario.

She was 34 years old when her husband passed away in 1922.

Mabel was 46 years old when the Dionne Quintuplets were born in 1934.

She was 58 years old when her father passed away in 1946.

Mabel was 79 years old when her sister, Isabel Rose Elizabeth, passed away in 1966.

She was 81 years old when she passed away in 1969.

GARRY BEARES[41]

Garry was an infant when he passed away. He is buried with his grandparents.

ALFRED FREDERICK BELL[42]

Alfred was born on August 1, 1864 in Kingston, Frontenac, Canada West, British Colonial America.

He was two years old when Ontario was founded on July 1, 1867.

Alfred was four years old when he passed away in 1869.

ALEXANDER HAY BELL[43]

Alexander was born on November 21, 1828.

He was 28 years old when he married Susannah Spooner on February 24, 1857 in Storrington, Ontario. His first child, John Alexander, passed away on October 28, 1857.

Alexander was 40 years old when his son, Alfred Frederick, passed away in 1896.

He was 42 years old when British Columbia joined the confederation in 1871.

Alexander was 43 years old when his father passed away in 1872.

He was 47 years old when his mother passed away in 1876.

Alexander was 49 years old when his brother, Francis, passed away in 1878.

He was 54 years old when the mining boom in northern Ontario began in 1883.

Alexander was 59 years old when his wife passed away in 1888.

He was 61 years old when his daughter, Jane Eleanor, passed away in 1890.

Alexander was 70 years old when his brother, James, passed away in 1899.

He was 79 years old when he passed away on April 22, 1908. Alexander was a Methodist farmer.

ALEXANDER WILLIAM BELL[44]

Alexander was born on August 12, 1877 in Montreal, Quebec.

He was five years old when the mining boom in northern Ontario began in 1883.

Alexander was 65 years old when the Conservate Party won the election in 1943.

He was 71 years old when he passed away in 1949.

CATHARINE (MOON) BELL[45]

Catharine was born in 1832.

She was 16 years old when her mother passed away in 1849.

Catharine was 17 years old when she married Francis Bell in 1850.

She was 31 years old when her father passed away in 1864.

Catharine was 33 years old when her brother, John Diamond, passed away in 1865.

She was 35 years old when Ontario was founded on July 1, 1867.

Catharine was 37 years old when her sister, Jane, passed away in 1870.

She was 38 years old when British Columbia joined the confederation in 1871.

Catharine was 41 years old when her sister, Mary Ann, passed away in 1874.

She was 45 years old when her husband passed away in 1878.

Catharine was 57 years old when her sister, Emily, passed away in 1889.

She was 68 years old when she passed away in 1900. Catharine was Methodist.

CHARLOTTE AMELIA (COWDY) BELL[46]

Charlotte was born in 1859.

She was five years old when her sister, Adeline, passed away in 1865.

Charlotte was 11 years old when British Columbia joined the confederation in 1871.

She was 25 years old when her son, John, passed away in 1885. Charlotte passed away on March 6th. She was Irish and Methodist.

DOROTHY JANE (WOOD) BELL[47]

Dorothy was born in 1866.

She was a year old when Ontario was founded on July 1, 1867.

Dorothy was five years old when British Columbia joined the confederation in 1871.

She was 12 years old when her brother, Wesley Herbert, passed away in 1878.

Dorothy was 17 years old when the mining boom began in northern Ontario in 1883.

She was 20 years old when she married Francis Wise in Brockville, Ontario on March 24, 1886.

Dorothy was 38 years old when her brother, Arthur Ernest, passed away in 1904.

She was 40 years old when her sister, Sarah Ann, passed away in 1907.

Dorothy was 44 years old when her husband passed away in 1910.

She was 46 years old when her father passed away in 1912.

Dorothy was 68 years old when the Dionne Quintuplets were born in 1934.

She was 71 years old when she passed away on October 2, 1937. Dorothy was Methodist.

EDNA (SNIDER) BELL[48]

Edna was born in 1898.

She was eight years old when Ontario Hydro was established in 1908.

Edna was 84 years old when she passed away in 1982.

ELIZABETH (BELL) RICHARDSON[49]

Elizabeth was born in 1924.

She was ten years old when the Dionne Quintuplets were born in 1934.

Elizabeth was 58 years old when the Canada Act was passed in 1982.

She was 76 years old when she passed away in 2000.

FRANCIS BELL[50]

Francis was born in 1824.

He was 26 years old when he married Catharine Moon in 1950.

Francis was 47 years old when British Columbia joined the confederation in 1971.

He was 48 years old when his father passed away in 1872.

Francis was 52 years old when his mother passed away in 1876.

He was 56 years old when he passed away in 1878.

FRANCIS WISE BELL[51]

Francis was born in 1854.

He was 13 years old when Ontario was founded on July 1, 1867.

Francis was 17 years old when British Columbia joined the confederation in 1871.

He was 24 years old when his father passed away in 1878.

Francis was 31 years old when his son, John, passed away in 1885. His wife, Charlotte Amelia, passed away the same year.

He was 32 years old when he married Dorothy Jane Wood on March 24, 1886 in Brockville, Ontario.

Francis was 46 years old when his mother passed away in 1900.

He was 47 years old when his sister, Catherine Mary, passed away in 1901.

Francis was 52 years old when Ontario Hydro was established in 1906.

He was 56 years old when he passed away in 1910.

GEORGE MAY BELL[52]

George was born on October 26, 1872 in Montreal, Quebec.

He was 10 years old when the mining boom in northern Ontario began in 1883.

George was 26 years old when his father passed away in 1899.

He was 33 years old when Ontario Hydro was established in 1906.

George was 37 years old when he married Laura Edna Davy in Odessa, Ontario on June 14, 1910.

He was 40 years old when his mother passed away in 1913.

George was 61 years old when he passed away on June 14, 1934. He is buried in Kingston. He was Methodist.

DR. GEORGE WESLEY BELL[53]

George was born in 1857.

He was nine years old when Ontario was founded on July 1, 1867.

George was 11 years old when his brother, Alfred Frederick, passed away in 1869.

He was 24 years old when he married Emma Bartley in 1882.

George was 25 years old when the mining boom in northern Ontario began in 1883.

He was 30 years old when his mother passed away in 1888.

George was 32 years old when his sister, Jane Eleanor, passed away in 1890.

He was 48 years old when Ontario Hydro was established in 1906.

George was 50 years old when his father passed away in 1908.

He was 51 years old when his wife passed away on June 29, 1909.

George was 52 years old when his sister, Mary Susannah, passed away in 1910. Thirteen months after his first wife's death, he married Lillian Florence Spooner on August 24, 1910. She was 24 years old.

He was 53 years old when his sister, Margaret Hannah, passed away in 1910.

George was 67 years old when he passed away on October 12, 1925.

HIRAM "EDWIN" BELL[54]

Edwin was born on March 26, 1890 in Frontenac, Ontario. His mother passed away on April 10th.

He was 15 years old when Ontario Hydro was established in 1906.

Edwin was 23 years old when he married Phyllis Elvira McDonald on October 29, 1913 in Collins Bay, Ontario.

He was 40 years old when his father passed away in 1931.

Edwin was 43 years old when the Dionne Quintuplets were born in 1934.

He was 46 years old when he passed away on July 30, 1936.

HARRY HAVELOCK BELL[55]

Harry passed away on September 9, 1885.

HELEN (ROBERTSON) BELL[56]

Helen passed away on January 25, 1901.

HELEN TABOR (STONE) BELL[57]

Helen was born in the USA in 1843.

She was 18 years old when she married John Bell on December 19, 1861 in Frontenac, Ontario.

Helen was 28 years old when British Columbia joined the confederation in 1871.

She was 56 years old when her husband passed away in 1899.

Helen was 63 years old when Ontario Hydro was established in 1906.

She was 70 years old when she passed away in 1913.

HIRAM EDWIN BELL[58]

Hiram was born on August 17, 1868 in Westbrook, Ontario.

He was less than a year old when his brother, Alfred Frederick, passed away in 1869.

Hiram was 14 years old when the mining boom in northern Ontario began in 1883.

He was 20 years old when he married Gretta Rose in Kingston, Township on April 23, 1889.

Hiram was 21 years old when his wife passed away on April 10, 1890. His sister, Jane Eleanor, passed away a month later on May 17th.

He was 37 years old when Ontario Hydro was established in 1906.

Hiram was 39 years old when his father passed away in 1908.

He was 41 years old when his sister, Mary Susannah, passed away in 1910.

Hiram was 42 years old when his sister, Margaret Hannah, passed away in 1910.

He was 57 years old when his brother, Dr. George Wesley Bell, passed away in 1925.

Hiram was 62 years old when he passed away in 1931. He was Methodist.

IDA M. (DUPLISSE) BELL[59]

Ida was born in 1872.

She was 18 years old when the Women's Suffrage movement began in 1890.

Ida was 19 years old when she married Hiram Bell on January 14, 1892 in Nashua, New Hampshire. She was his second wife.

Ida was 59 years old when her husband passed away in 1931.

She was 62 years old when the Dionne Quintuplets were born in 1934.

Ida was 90 years old when she passed away in 1962.

JAMES BELL[60]

James was born on December 20, 1838 in Kingston, Ontario.

He was 23 years old when he married Helen Tabor Stone on December 19, 1861 in Frontenac, Ontario.

James was 28 years old when Ontario was founded on July 1, 1867.

He was 32 years old when British Columbia joined the confederation in 1871.

James was 33 years old when his father passed away in 1872.

He was 37 years old when his mother passed away in 1876.

James was 39 years old when his brother, Francis, passed away in 1878.

He was 44 years old when the mining boom in northern Ontario began in 1883.

James was 60 years old when he passed away on May 15, 1899.

JAMES G. BELL[61]

James was born in 1864.

He was three years old when Ontario was founded on July 1, 1867.

James was seven years old when British Columbia joined the confederation in 1871.

He was 50 years old when he passed away in 1899.

JOHN BELL[62]

John passed away on March 29, 1900.

JOHN B. BELL[63]

John was born in England in 1798.

He was two years old when the Act of Union was passed in 1801.

John was 24 years old when Rugby Football was invented in 1823.

He was 25 years old when he married Margaret Hays on January 20, 1824 in Nafferton, England.

John was 44 years old when "A Christmas Carol" was first published in 1843.

He was 68 years old when Ontario was founded on July 1, 1847.

John was 73 years old when he passed away on June 4, 1872.

KATHERINE LUCINDA (THOMPSON) BELL[64]

Katherine was born in 1887.

She was 19 years old when Ontario Hydro was established in 1906.

Katherine was 57 years old when she passed away in 1944.

KENNETH M. BELL[65]

Kenneth was born in 1881.

He was two years old when the mining boom in northern Ontario began in 1883.

Kenneth was 25 years old when Ontario Hydro was established in 1906.

He was 44 years old when he passed away in 1925.

LYLE BELL[66]

Lyle is buried in Kingston. I believe he may have been an infant, however, more research is needed. Please see the footnote if you'd like to help.

MARGARET (HALF) BELL[67]

Margaret was born on April 9, 1795.

She was 71 years old when Ontario was founded on July 1, 1867.

Margaret was 74 years old when she passed away on February 10, 1870.

MARGARET HANNAH (BELL) FINNIGAN[68]

Margaret was born in 1866 in Westbrook, Kingston, Ontario. She was a year old when Ontario was founded on July 1, 1867.

Margaret was three years old when her brother, Alfred Frederick, passed away in 1869.

She was 17 years old when the mining boom in northern Ontario began in 1883.

Margaret was 20 years old when the Statue of Liberty was dedicated in 1886.

She was 22 years old when her mother passed away in 1888.

Margaret was 24 years old when the Sherman Antitrust Act was passed in 1890. Her sister, Jane Eleanor, also passed away that year.

She was 29 years old when she married James Oswald Finnigan on September 2, 1896 in Kingston, Ontario. He was 22 years old.

Margaret was 40 years old when Ontario Hydro was established in 1906.

She was 42 years old when her father passed away in 1908.

Margaret was 44 years old when the Mann Act was passed in 1910. Her sister, Mary Susannah, also passed away that year.

She was 45 years old when she passed away on December 25, 1910.

O. BLANCHE BELL[69]

It is uncertain when Blanche was born or died. If you'd like to help, please check out the footnote. Thank you.

PANSY WINONA BELL[70]

Pansy was born in Brockville, Ontario on July 17, 1889.

She was 16 years old when Ontario Hydro was established in 1906.

Pansy was 20 years old when she passed away in 1910.

SIDANNA MAY (DAVY) BELL[71]

Sidanna was born on May 25, 1877 in Hawkesbury, Prescott, Ontario. She was five years old when the mining boom in northern Ontario began in 1883.

Sidanna was 22 years old when she married Alexander Wood Bell in 1900.

She was 28 years old when Ontario Hydro was established in 1906.

Sidanna was 32 years old when her sister, Nellie Louise, passed away in 1909.

She was 56 years old when her father passed away in 1933.

Sidanna was 64 years old when her mother passed away in 1941.

She was 69 years old when her sister, Eliza Jane Carmina, passed away in 1947.

Sidanna was 70 years old when her sister, Katherine Henrietta, passed away in 1948.

She was 72 years old when her husband passed away in 1949.

Sidanna was 73 years old when her brother, Henry Anthony Mowatt, passed away in 1950.

She was 77 years old when she passed away on June 18, 1954.

SUSANNAH (SPOONER) BELL[72]

Susannah was born in 1833.

She was nine years old when her brother, John, passed away in 1842.

Susannah was 24 years old when she married Alexander Hay Bell on February 24, 1857. Their first child, John Alexander, passed away on October 20th.

She was 31 years old when her mother passed away in 1864.

Susannah was 33 years old when her father passed away in 1866.

She was 36 years old when her son, Alfred Frederick, passed away in 1869.

Susannah was 38 years old when her brother, George, passed away in 1871.

She was 50 years old when the mining boom in northern Ontario began in 1883.

Susannah was 53 years old when the Statue of Liberty was dedicated in 1886.

She was 54 years old when her brother, John Crawford, passed away in 1887.

Susannah was 55 years old when she passed away in 1888. She was German/Irish and Methodist.

THOMAS WOOD BELL[73]

Thomas was born on July 30, 1891 in Frontenac, Ontario.

He was 14 years old when Ontario Hydro was established in 1906.

Thomas was 18 years old when both of his parents passed away in 1910.

He was 24 years old when he married Katherine Lucy Thompson on June 15, 1916 in Kingston, Ontario.

Thomas was 42 years old when the Dionne Quintuplets were born in 1934.

He was 52 years old when his wife passed away in 1944.

Thomas was 58 years old when his daughter, Loiuse Frances, passed away in 1949.

He was 63 years old when his son, Ashford Wood, passed away in 1955.

Thomas was 71 years old when he passed away in 1963.

WILLIAM HENRY BELL[74]

William was born on September 13, 1862 in Westbrook, Ontario. He was four years old when Ontario was founded on July 1, 1867.

William was six years old when his brother, Alfred Frederick, passed away in 1869.

He was eight years old when British Columbia joined the confederation in 1871.

William was 20 years old when he passed away in 1882.

---

[1] https://www.wikitree.com/genealogy/Saunders-Family-Tree-13522

[2] https://www.wikitree.com/genealogy/Appleton-Family-Tree-1770

[3] https://www.wikitree.com/genealogy/Appleton-Family-Tree-1771

[4] https://www.wikitree.com/genealogy/Appleton-Family-Tree-1772

[5] https://www.wikitree.com/genealogy/Appleton-Family-Tree-1773

[6] https://www.wikitree.com/genealogy/Appleton-Family-Tree-1774

[7] https://www.wikitree.com/genealogy/Claxton-Family-Tree-1016

[8] https://www.wikitree.com/genealogy/Appleton-Family-Tree-1775

[9] https://www.wikitree.com/genealogy/Arseneth-Family-Tree-1

[10] https://www.wikitree.com/genealogy/Ash-Family-Tree-3844

[11] https://www.wikitree.com/genealogy/Breden-Family-Tree-106

[12] https://www.wikitree.com/genealogy/Ashley-Family-Tree-5572

[13] https://www.wikitree.com/genealogy/Ashley-Family-Tree-5573

[14] https://www.wikitree.com/genealogy/Burnett-Family-Tree-4900

[15] https://www.wikitree.com/genealogy/Ashley-Family-Tree-5575

[16] https://www.wikitree.com/genealogy/Ashley-Family-Tree-3789

[17] https://www.wikitree.com/genealogy/Ashley-Family-Tree-5574

[18] https://www.wikitree.com/genealogy/Asselstine-Family-Tree-78

[19] https://www.wikitree.com/genealogy/Fleming-Family-Tree-14018

[20] https://www.wikitree.com/genealogy/Jackson-Family-Tree-31078

[21] https://www.wikitree.com/genealogy/Asselstine-Family-Tree-72

[22] https://www.wikitree.com/genealogy/Atkins-Family-Tree-5105

[23] https://www.wikitree.com/genealogy/Atkinson-Family-Tree-7820

[24] https://www.wikitree.com/genealogy/Silver-Family-Tree-575

[25] https://www.wikitree.com/genealogy/Aylesworth-Family-Tree-133

[26] https://www.wikitree.com/genealogy/Aylesworth-Family-Tree-378

[27] https://www.wikitree.com/genealogy/Aylesworth-Family-Tree-379

[28] https://www.wikitree.com/genealogy/Zurbrigg-Family-Tree-15

[29] https://www.wikitree.com/genealogy/David-Family-Tree-2668

[30] https://www.wikitree.com/genealogy/Aylesworth-Family-Tree-139

[31] https://www.wikitree.com/genealogy/Aylesworth-Family-Tree-380

[32] https://www.wikitree.com/genealogy/Aylesworth-Family-Tree-263

[33] https://www.findagrave.com/memorial/113991331/wilbert-ross-aylesworth

[34] https://www.wikitree.com/genealogy/Babcock-Family-Tree-8450

[35] https://www.wikitree.com/genealogy/Day-Family-Tree-19281

[36] https://www.wikitree.com/genealogy/Baker-Family-Tree-59606

[37] https://www.wikitree.com/genealogy/Cairns-Family-Tree-2116

[38] https://www.wikitree.com/genealogy/Baker-Family-Tree-59617

[39] https://www.wikitree.com/genealogy/Baker-Family-Tree-44138

[40] https://www.wikitree.com/genealogy/David-Family-Tree-3172

[41] https://www.wikitree.com/genealogy/Beares-Family-Tree-15

[42] https://www.wikitree.com/genealogy/Bell-Family-Tree-38667

[43] https://www.wikitree.com/genealogy/Bell-Family-Tree-38668

[44] https://www.wikitree.com/genealogy/Bell-Family-Tree-38670

[45] https://www.wikitree.com/genealogy/Moon-Family-Tree-5774

[46] https://www.wikitree.com/genealogy/Cowdy-Family-Tree-16

[47] https://www.wikitree.com/genealogy/Wood-Family-Tree-35071

[48] https://www.wikitree.com/genealogy/Snider-Family-Tree-3282

[49] https://www.wikitree.com/genealogy/Bell-Family-Tree-28298

[50] https://www.wikitree.com/genealogy/Bell-Family-Tree-28296

[51] https://www.wikitree.com/genealogy/Bell-Family-Tree-28294

[52] https://www.wikitree.com/genealogy/Bell-Family-Tree-38673

[53] https://www.wikitree.com/genealogy/Bell-Family-Tree-38674

[54] https://www.wikitree.com/genealogy/Bell-Family-Tree-32907

[55] https://www.wikitree.com/genealogy/Bell-Family-Tree-38676

[56] https://www.wikitree.com/genealogy/Robertson-Family-Tree-25697

[57] https://www.wikitree.com/genealogy/Stone-Family-Tree-25054

[58] https://www.wikitree.com/genealogy/Bell-Family-Tree-38677

[59] https://www.wikitree.com/genealogy/Duplisse-Family-Tree-3

[60] https://www.wikitree.com/genealogy/Bell-Family-Tree-38678

[61] https://www.wikitree.com/genealogy/Bell-Family-Tree-38681

[62] https://www.wikitree.com/genealogy/Bell-Family-Tree-38682

[63] https://www.wikitree.com/genealogy/Bell-Family-Tree-38683

[64] https://www.wikitree.com/genealogy/Thompson-Family-Tree-77926

[65] https://www.wikitree.com/genealogy/Bell-Family-Tree-38684

[66] https://www.wikitree.com/genealogy/Bell-Family-Tree-38685

[67] https://www.wikitree.com/genealogy/Half-Family-Tree-7

[68] https://www.wikitree.com/genealogy/Bell-Family-Tree-38213

[69] https://www.wikitree.com/genealogy/Bell-Family-Tree-38697

[70] https://www.wikitree.com/genealogy/Bell-Family-Tree-28295

[71] https://www.wikitree.com/genealogy/Davy-Family-Tree-1995

[72] https://www.wikitree.com/genealogy/Spooner-Family-Tree-2303

[73] https://www.wikitree.com/genealogy/Bell-Family-Tree-28297

[74] https://www.wikitree.com/genealogy/Bell-Family-Tree-38699

Don't miss out!

Visit the website below and you can sign up to receive emails whenever Angeline Gallant publishes a new book. There's no charge and no obligation.

https://books2read.com/r/B-A-QGSI-UULBC

BOOKS 2 READ

Connecting independent readers to independent writers.

Also by Angeline Gallant

Calling Her Heart
Whisper of the Heart
No Turning Back
Forsake Me Not
Hear My Cry

Keeper Of Secrets
A Lady's Secret

Midnight's Awakening
Heart of the Storm
Walking Through The Storm

Secrets of the Underworld
Deklan's Dragons

Tell My Story Collection

Tell My Story: England 1852

The Grave Whisperer

Wedding Bells in Kingston, Ontario, Canada 1923

St. Paul's Anglican Churchyard Kingston, Ontario, Canada A-B

St. Paul's Anglican Churchyard, Kingston, Ontario, Canada C - D

St. Paul's Anglican Churchyard, Kingston, Ontario, Canada G - H

St. Paul's Anglican Churchyard, Kingston, Ontario, Canada J - N

St. Paul's Anglican Churchyard, Kingston, Ontario, Canada O - R

St. Paul's Anglican Churchyard, Kingston, Ontario, Canada S - T

St. Paul's Anglican Churchyard, Kingston, Ontario T - Z

Small Graveyards & Burial Grounds: Kingston, Ontario, Canada

Cataraqui United Church Cemetery 1

The Wolf Whisperer Series

The Cry of the Wolf

Journey of the Heart

Wolf Whisperer volumes 1 & 2

Standalone

Winds of Change vol 1-3

Watch for more at https://www.goodreads.com/author/show/19703964.Angeline_Gallant.

www.ingramcontent.com/pod-product-compliance
Ingram Content Group UK Ltd.
Pitfield, Milton Keynes, MK11 3LW, UK
UKHW021655190726
13853UKWH00001B/283

9 798215 698310